Travelling the Silk Road

Silk Road

A Journey on the Orient Silk Road Express

Jolyn Jones

Portia Publishing

For Tadzik and Posy who inspired this book

CONTENTS

CHAPTER ONE

The Silk Road

In those far-off school days who was not beguiled by James Elroy Flecker's poem 'The Golden Journey to Samarkand' with its promise of oriental travel across the desert sands to the fabled city of golden spires? It must be one of the most famous journeys of all time to travel the ancient Silk Road along which silk, paper and spices and other exotic goods were transported across deserts by camel trains from China to the West.

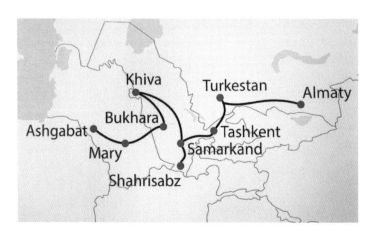

Its origins date to the second century BC when Emperor Wu of China found his land constantly under attack from the marauding nomadic Xiongnu tribe who were fabled horsemen. Wu wanted more horses to repel the invaders so sent out an emissary to find a new source of horses and seek allies in the fight against the invaders. The emissary returned with news of a country which had rice, wheat and grapes and also 'heavenly' horses. This was Ferghana, or what is now known as Uzbekistan.

China was unique in being able to produce silk, the production of which was a closely guarded secret. So silk was what the Emperor had to trade. While the heavenly horses (about which a war was later fought) were good for battle, camels were the beasts used for carrying goods across the deserts of Central Asia to the main trading centres. Gradually many kinds of goods, spices and animals were traded, knowledge, ideas and religion soon followed along with the inevitable transmission of diseases.

The network of routes began in China and ran to the Mediterranean and varied over time, season and tribal control. Its great days were over by the end of the 1400's when the sea routes via the Cape of Good Hope offered faster and cheaper transport between Europe and India and the Far East. In the days of Camels (desert) and Yaks (mountain passes), it was reckoned that goods took eight months to traverse the Silk Road.

The Chinese are currently investing in rail transport along the Old Silk Road as a faster way to move their goods to Europe as an alternative to Air (expensive), Sea (slow) and the Trans-Siberian (Russian controlled and congested).

Following the Silk Road requires a long journey across Central Asia and we opted to join a private train trip across Turkmenistan, Uzbekistan and Kazakhstan covering 2548 miles. It is possible to do it by bus or shared taxi, but the roads are terrible. Likewise, it can be done by plane hopping from place to place. The train seemed the most straightforward option. We flew to Turkmenistan, the least known and least visited of the countries of Central Asia. Some describe it as a totalitarian theme park, but that is to do it a great disservice. It has ancient cities such as Merv, important to both the Silk Road and to the later development of Islam. Merv was once ranked along with Damascus, Baghdad and Cairo as a great trading city. The country is vast and bordered by Uzbekistan, Kazakhstan, Afghanistan and Iran. Much of the country is occupied by the Karakum desert which has now yielded abundant gas and some oil.

We arrived in Ashgabat, capital of Turkmenistan, around midnight. We had not been looking forward to it as officialdom in this country demands that you apply on landing for a permit to enter the airport before being allowed to join the Immigration queues. It is a lengthy and solemn procedure only enlivened by our first sight of the dress of Turkmenistan women who 'man' the checkpoints. Their headdresses are spectacular and very fetching. The male officials wear those high peaked caps which we associate with Russia or former East Germany from all those Cold War spy films. We have arrived in a different world.

After being duly processed at the airport we are divided into small groups of up to fifteen sorted by Tour Company or common language, and there are coaches or buses for the designated groups, ours is Red. It makes it easy to identify which vehicle we are supposed to be on. To our surprise, the drive to the hotel is turned into an 'Ashgabat by Night' tour at two o clock in the morning. It presents a very strange sight as the well-spaced tall buildings are spectacularly lit by colour changing lights. If you think of London's Shard and Gherkin buildings, then you will begin to get the picture only here there are many of them in fantastic shapes that glow in the dark. To say that they are spectacular doesn't really paint the picture well enough. One is like a skull grinning at us in the dark as it slowly changes from green to yellow and runs through the colour spectrum.

Plus of course there are the monuments, they are in honour of either the First President or the current President since Ashgabat counts its heroes only from independence in 1991. It is all reminiscent of how Rome must have looked when an Emperor ordered another triumphal arch to be built to celebrate a victory, real or imaginary. A touch of Disneyland here too.

Finally, we arrive at our hotel which is a towering building shaped like a hitchhikers thumb, lit by colour changing lights of course. The bedrooms are spectacular and are the largest and most luxurious that we have ever seen, this is going to make the transfer to a small train compartment later in the day all the more difficult. We are due to leave at 8.30 (no weaklings allowed on this trip), and it is now 3.00 so not much time to enjoy the hotel amenities. No surprise there.

CHAPTER TWO

Ashgabat

Ashgabat, the capital of Turkmenistan, was devastated by an earthquake in 1948 which destroyed the city and killed two-thirds of the population. It was rebuilt by the Soviets, but since independence in 1991, most of the Soviet buildings have been demolished, and the new architect designed city has been built. The country is one of the largest producers of natural gas and oil in the world, and its considerable wealth derives from this. The First President decreed that its citizens should be provided with free gas and water and every family was given a plot of land on which to build a home. The ordinary housing consists of a single storey rectangular box with a corrugated iron roof. In the city, there are gigantic apartment blocks, presumably the preserve of the good and the great.

In daylight, the city looks as spectacularly beautiful as at night. Without exception, everything is white marble with gold domes, and Ashgabat claims to have more marble-clad buildings than any other city in the world. There are plenty of parks with trees which have yet to reach full growth. This is a desert city with an extreme climate reaching 40 to 50 degrees in summer and minus 30 in winter, although sometimes even colder.

Although the President is elected by popular vote, it is an authoritarian regime. To give some bizarre examples, private black

cars were banned from the roads, apparently because the President considered them unlucky. Citizens with black cars had to get them repainted white or have them seized and pay a large fine. Strangely official cars are still black. The Interior Minister has now taken against women drivers alleging that they are responsible for most of the car accidents. While there is not yet an outright ban they are doing their best to intimidate women from driving by every means possible. The current president has pronounced that the free gas, electricity and water provided to citizens by his predecessor is under review, clearly not enough in the bank to build all the new monuments he would like. There is little crime because the penalties are so harsh.

Turkmenistan, with a population of around 5,130,000, is the fifth largest gas supplier in the world but it is a landlocked country (barring the Caspian Sea) and in the last two years its pipelines through Russia have been blocked. It is desperately seeking new markets in Western China and in India (requiring a pipeline through Afghanistan!) so the government income has been severely cut.

Our first stop on today's tour is the site of the ancient Parthian city of Nisa, the archaeological remains of which are now a World Heritage site.

Fortunately, the meticulous organisation of our trip is immediately clear as only our small group is there at this amazing place. A site guide takes us around and brings the mud-walled ruins to life for us so we can imagine the water courses, temples and what life was like behind the protection of the city walls and how they were defended against attackers. Excavations have revealed large buildings, mausoleums and shrines believed to be for the cult of Zarathustr, who were fire worshippers. The cult is still followed in remote parts of the region, and some rituals have been absorbed into later religions. Many Greek influences are apparent as a result of the incursions of Alexander the Great.

Nisa was totally destroyed by an earthquake which occurred in the first decade BC. The treasures unearthed in the archaeological digs are in the museum in Ashgabat. The city stood at the crossroads of various

Silk Road routes, but it is difficult to imagine its one-time importance while standing in an otherwise empty landscape viewing the remains of the desert city in intense heat.

Then we moved from ancient to modern as we drove to the white and gold mausoleum of the First President, still guarded by troops, whether these are to stop him from escaping or the citizens from defacing it is not clear. This is our first mausoleum on the trip and next to it is our first mosque. Large, modern, gilded and incredibly ornate, it is outside of the city so difficult for the faithful to attend in large numbers. We discard our shoes and venturing inside on to the carpets are invited to sit on the floor for a lecture. Given our average age of mid-seventies, we all find getting down to sit on the floor difficult and getting up again even more taxing. Afterwards, we are invited to use their very clean toilet facilities, and this is our first experience of 'squatters'. Most decline the offer.

The afternoon is spent touring monuments of Ashgabat, all in white and gold with the occasional black lines accentuating them. Amongst the more bizarre is the 'Arch of Neutrality,' a 75metre high rocket-shaped tower with a golden statue of the First President at the top. The statue at first rotated so that his face was always in the sun but for some reason no longer does so. Built to celebrate the President's decision to adopt neutrality the monument cost over $12,000,000. Amongst the new government buildings the Ministry of Gas is shaped like a cigarette lighter, but like most government buildings it is forbidden to photograph it. There is even a Ministry of Fairness, although what that was all about was not explained.

We finish at the National Museum which houses the relics found at Nisa, and it is stuffed full of antiquities made less interesting by the fact that we are not allowed to just look and read the descriptions but have to have an enthusiastic guide explain everything to us in full. It has been a very long day, and we are all tired and one by one we drift away and sit outside in the sunshine.

At last, it is time to join the train, and we are soon on board trying hard to fit our luggage into our tiny compartment. Ingenuity is required for this but at last, everything has a place, and in line with the onboard radio announcements we are allocated a dining car and time for meals.

Our dining car is rich in polished wood, comfortable armchairs, silken hangings, white tablecloths, and sparkling glasses. We sit within an area allocated for our red group, but the blue group also share our restaurant car. They are principally an exuberant Brazilian group, all speaking excellent English of course, with a well-travelled Norwegian couple plus another British couple. It is a relief when it is time for bed as there has been precious little sleep since leaving home.

First night on the train and the bunks are reasonably sized and comfortable, but while we normally think of trains having a soporific rhythm, this one does not. It is more like sleeping in a sieve that is constantly being shaken, and that's before the train shunts in the middle of the night to change engines or whatever. It will take some getting used to.

CHAPTER THREE

Merv – Queen of the World

It is a relief to get up and get showered and dressed, one at a time of course as when the bunks are down there is only room for one person to stand. The walk to the restaurant car for breakfast involves moving between several swaying carriages with many trip hazards. I take a seat opposite a man who is waiting for his wife and chat about the difficulties of sleeping on a train. They have come via Istanbul and reached Ashgabat earlier than we did so did a tour of all the monuments, mosques and museums on arrival, and then did them all again with the official party. His wife, when she arrives, says that she has already seen more monuments than she ever wanted to, what her heart is set on is purchasing a silk carpet. My husband joins us, and after breakfast, we go and get ready to leave for the day as we have already arrived at Merv.

When we get back to our cabin, which has been restored to its daytime configuration, my husband says 'Did you realise that was…' (Naming a one-time party leader and a household name.) No, I didn't, but I thought his face looked vaguely familiar.

We leave the train at 8.30, the heat is still intense, and it is going to get hotter as the day goes on.

It looks as though there is full employment in Turkmenistan as ladies are employed to sweep all the roads with besoms throughout the day. Gardeners line the landscaped roundabouts titivating them and are still at work when we return hours later. We are a bit mystified as to why we have a police escort fore and aft and sweep through traffic lights and other obstructions.

The roundabout gardeners stand to attention and salute as we pass. Is this the normal way they treat visitors to Turkmenistan?

Our first stop is the ruins of Merv, it is a vast site, and we need the coach to transport us from one part to another. In ancient times Merv was known as 'The Queen of the World' and was a major trading hub for the Silk Road. It ranked alongside Damascus, Baghdad and Cairo as one of the greatest cities in the Islamic world. There were actually five cities of Merv as over the centuries it suffered destruction by an attack or simply the shifting course of the rivers which supplied it. So each new city was built alongside the old one. Merv is thought to be the inspiration for Scheherazade's 'Thousand and One Nights.'

Finally, Merv was completely destroyed in 1221 by one of Ghengis Khan's sons, Tolui, who arrived with an army of thousands following the city's refusal to either pay substantial taxes or surrender the city's most beautiful young women to Ghengis Khan. Tolui accepted the peaceful surrender of the city but once through the city gates his army slaughtered all the city's 300,000 inhabitants and Merv was no more.

The first part of the site consists of two forts with substantial walls rising out of the arid desert. They can be seen from miles away and must have been a spectacular sight to early travellers. This part was supposed to be where the young women of the city lived. More than a stone's throw away there was another part where the young unmarried men lived, and there is a legend about a contest to see if they could throw an apple into the women's quarters to claim a bride. It would be an Olympian throw, and it is claimed that this led to the development of the slingshot.

We then climb up a steep hill to view the old city walls. It looks exactly like a bomb crater but if you squeeze your eyes half shut you can visualise what it once looked like, a magnificent city teeming with life.

Other monuments and mausoleums abound, and many are the object of pilgrimages such as those built for two Askhabs or standard bearers of the Prophet Muhammed. These belong to al-Hakim Ibn Amr al-Jifari and Buraida ibn al-Huseib a-Asami who lived in the seventh century. Behind the mausoleums is a pair of portals of the Timurid period (15th century.) This is where we learn of the practices of modern pilgrims to these holy places. The women walk all around a mausoleum touching the surface and are said to gain energy from this and can ask for blessings on themselves or sick relatives. The men visit but don't touch. There is a working ancient water cistern close by, a miracle of the desert. As we have been banned from using the bug-laden water from taps in Turkmenistan, we don't risk putting our hands in the water cistern.

There are many more sights to see on the complex with the mausoleum at Sultan Kala being one of the most imposing. It was built to honour Sultan Sanjar and was said to be visible a day's ride away across the steppes. The architect, whose name is etched on the building, was executed to prevent him from ever designing a more imposing building. Clearly, recent Presidents of Turkmenistan are following a precedent – if you're going to build a monument or mausoleum build it as high as you can and make it as dramatic as possible. Not sure whether they still deal with architects in the same way.

We can also see a 12th-century mosque on the site which was built around the tomb of a 12th-century dervish, but it is not open to non-Muslims. But enough of monuments, mausoleums and mosques, it is time for lunch with a Turkmen family.

That isn't quite what we get as lunch for the entire party is served at long tables in a covered area which looks like a village community centre. There is music being played to stimulate the appetite, and we examine the food which covers the tables with great interest. There are sharing plates of salad, and also dishes of sweetmeats which we assume are for the end of the meal, but we've got that wrong, they are intended to 'open the appetite' at the beginning of the meal. Soup is served, and it is a clear soup with lots of bits in it. It is less than delicious but that doesn't matter, the aim is for an authentic experience. An indeterminate main course follows, and we soon discover that two of our group have special dietary needs which colour all our mealtimes. A meal always finishes with black or green tea served in cups without handles, that is if our guide isn't trying to rush us to get going and visit the next mausoleum or whatever.

Then we are off back to the train, past the same gardeners and sweeping ladies still at work. What clothes do locals wear? Turkmen ladies wear an everyday dress of a richly embroidered coat type dress over embroidered trousers. Their headdresses, again embroidered, cover the hair but not the face. No-one wears the Muslim style of headgear that we have become familiar with in the UK. Men wear long black coats with a square embroidered hat, and young men wear western-style clothing.

We have passed several wedding palaces during the day, and our guide explains that Turkmens don't do living together, they must get married first, and this is always a very big occasion. A dowry is paid, and guests at the wedding will be at least three or four hundred people and often up to a thousand, it sounds very expensive. It is an accepted practise for marriages to be arranged although more liberal parents may

allow their children a free choice. Our guide, who is in his thirties, is unmarried and still resisting parental pressure.

We have a long train journey to reach the Uzbekistan border and then a further lengthy journey to Bukhara. On the train, we have a rare opportunity to socialise with our neighbours in the compartments in our carriage, there being no observation car or communal area, just a narrow corridor. Much is made in the brochures of the chance to sit and watch the view from our compartments, but the scenery of continuous scrubby desert isn't the most alluring, in fact, it is positively sleeping inducing.

At dinner, our indefatigable tour director, Anke, explains that there are ninety-seven passengers on the train from thirteen countries or was it seventeen? The common factor is an ability to speak English or German and an interest in the ancient Silk Route. The nationalities include Germans, Brazilians, Norwegians, Chinese, Singaporeans, Australians and Canadians as well as British. Our police escort is also explained because we have the Deputy Prime Minister of a South East Asian country holidaying with us and he and his entourage occupy half of the carriage that we are in. He is the tall, pleasant gentleman two compartments up from us. After this, we do tend to notice that our carriage is guarded on the outside whenever we stop at any station.

And now we have left Turkmenistan behind and are in Uzbekistan.

CHAPTER FOUR

Bukhara

Our tour director instructs us over the radio 'When you hear the music get off the train.' The train has actually been sitting in Bukhara station for an hour or two, so not a busy line. The station itself is a typical Russian monolith with lots of blue reflective glass and many officials milling about the platform. The music is provided by a group of musicians playing local instruments which to our ears sound excruciating. Worst is the six-foot-long trumpets which only seem to be able to produce one long discordant note, repeatedly. We descend from the train clutching our overnight cases – the next two nights we will stay in Bukhara hotels.

As we are in a new country, we have new local guides, compulsory for visiting these ex-Soviet countries, visitors are not allowed to wander about unsupervised. One chap with a worried expression is waving a red flag, so we reassure him that the red group is all present even if we are not surrounding him like a flock of geese.

Next, a local strongman provides entertainment by lifting impossible weights first with his arms and then with his teeth and all to background music. Weightlifting must be very popular in Uzbekistan. At last, having applauded the show, we are free to leave the platform, and exit to the waiting minibuses.

It is very hot even though it is still quite early and we are deposited in a park which surrounds many of the monuments, mausoleums, museums, medressas, minarets and mosques of Bukhara. We flit from one bit of shade to another while our guide lectures us about the history of the city which was regarded as a holy place from pre-Christian times and is now said to be Central Asia's holiest city.

We cannot be alone in never having heard of medrassas before, there are various spellings of this word, but they are or were educational institutes whether religious or secular. Many are now craft centres, and some were caravanserai before being converted to medrassas. They are spectacular buildings like all the 'M's' that we visit from now on. These highly decorated buildings are what most people have in mind when they think of the ancient Silk Routes, and we will be visiting them in confusing profusion from now on.

First up is the Samanid family Mausoleum and it is said that Ismail himself was buried here in 907. It is a classic Islamic cube crowned with a dome and ornate decoration inside and out. Then on to the Chasma-Ayub which is on the site where Job struck the earth with his staff and made a healing well or chasma. It is now a museum of water for want of a better description.

Up to the 19th century Bukhara had many canals and stone pools as an oasis city, and these were where people gathered, gossiped, washed and bathed. They became a prime source of infection and plague, and because of this, the average life of a Bukhara citizen was only 32 years. The Russians invaded in 1868, and when the Bolsheviks took control, they drained the pools and put in a new water system.

Then it is back to our minibus to take us to the Royal Fort which is situated on a hilltop. This was the home of successive emirs ending with the one known as 'the Butcher' who murdered all his brothers and twenty-eight relatives to take the throne. He achieved infamy in the western world by executing two British Officers after keeping them in a pit filled with snakes and scorpions for more than four years. His enormous robes and those of his wives are on display, but there is only a model of his sumptuous throne, the original having been seized and taken to Moscow. Many tourists are visiting the Fort today, but we are the only Western visitors. The country is now encouraging its own citizens to go and see all its historic sites, and these 'local' tourists are visiting in great numbers. They all stare at us in amazement, unfamiliar with westerners and western dress. Let's face it, our dress is pretty shabby compared to theirs.

We are now in a pattern of visiting sites from 8.30 to 1.30, an hour for lunch, and then more tourist attractions from 2.30 to 5.30. It is heavy going with no coffee breaks and no toilet stops. Public toilets are few, and according to the guidebook most toilets are awful and the rest worse. Those of our party who do visit them come out to find the group has vanished. Fortunately, we occasionally pause for a count to see if we are all there. There are fourteen of us which for some reason our guide refers to as 'seven', so the answer to everything becomes 'seven.'

All the M's follow thick and fast, we are clearly going to visit everyone last one of them in the city, and there are plenty of them, but we will be here for another day and a half. At last, we see the beautiful blue or azure domes and intricate majolica tiling everywhere, it is mesmerisingly beautiful, but the light is not at its best for photographs as the weather is looking threatening.

Reaching our hotel at 5.30, we have a short time to shower and change before going out to dinner. The hotel is quite basic, and the rooms are small although at least bigger than our train cabins.

Too soon we are off again for our evening meal with a preceding visit to a silk shop. The restaurant is glitzy with revolving lights lighting a catwalk for a silk fashion show. The fashion show is quite interesting and would be more so if any of us had any resemblance to a model's shape.

There is also very loud live modern Uzbeck music as a background to dining and the fashion show. The meal follows the usual format of salad, soup with indeterminate bits in it, the main course and the dessert is a popular local dish called 'Chak chak.' It consists of something that looks like popcorn or a breakfast cereal welded into an industrial lump with honey and other syrupy goo. A teaspoon is provided for eating it. I attempt to break into it, and after chipping away, a large lump soars into the air and flies over my shoulder not to be seen again until I tread on it on the way out. A fitting end to the evening.

CHAPTER FIVE

Holy Sites of Bukhara

It has rained overnight and is a much more pleasant 20° which is a bit of a surprise after it has been so hot. The first visit today is to the mausoleum of Sheikh Boharzi who founded a Sufi community here and was a poet, mystic and theologist. It is considered a very holy place and a visit here is for some an alternative to a journey to Mecca. Sheikh Boharzi was also a noted embroiderer in gold work, still a speciality of the region.

While our guide is telling us all this, we are gathered in a courtyard by the tomb, and a constant stream of visitors are praying by it. They cannot touch the tomb as they would like to because it is protected by a small moat. We seemed to have been rooted to the spot for a while, and gradually visitors start pushing themselves in amongst us, not because they resent us taking up valuable space but because they want their friends to photograph them with us or to take a selfie.

We had been instructed not to take photos of people without their permission, but that doesn't seem to hold good the other way round, and we are surrounded with visitors who want to take pictures of us, or with us. None of us is exactly photogenic, but here we are featuring in dozens of photographs, presumably because we are something of an oddity. Our guide says that locals like to have their photos taken with us because it will bring good fortune and that our photos will take pride of place in their homes. Well, that's a polite way of putting it.

From hereon cameras snap at us, and we are dragged into group photos to smile inanely at the cameras of complete strangers. There is nothing to do but cooperate wholeheartedly, even though we hate having our photographs taken. There are not many family groups, it tends to be a gaggle of girls or a group of mature ladies who look like a mothers union outing or even a lively group of young men or a romantic couple. We smile and pose for them all. Bizarre isn't in it.

Some time is spent exploring all the mausoleums and mosques on the site which sit in a well laid out garden. Builders are repairing a wall, and they don't just have a flask of tea like at home, but a china teapot and cup.

The ladies of our party also explore the various stalls selling beautifully embroidered jackets, and some make their first purchase. We all agree that there is unlikely to be any event back home to which we could wear these garments, but that doesn't seem a sufficient reason not to buy one.

Next stop is the Sultan's Summer Palace out in the countryside away from the summer heat of the city. As it was built after the country had become an annexe of Russia, there is a distinctly Russian influence in the architecture. The interior is cool and very ornate.

Elsewhere the quarters for the Sultan's wives have a tranquil pool for them to bathe in with an ornate platform a short distance away for the Sultan to view the scene. He could make his choice of a nighttime companion by lobbing an apple into the pool to see who caught it. Apples seemed to play a prominent part in life in Central Asia.

After lunch, there are more mosques, medrassas, mausoleums and mosaics to wonder at. It is all becoming quite bewildering. The sun has left us, and it is cooler, which is something of a relief.

Back in Bokhara, we visit first a synagogue and then a silk carpet factory. In the workroom, girls sit on the floor or on cushions to weave the carpets. It doesn't look comfortable sitting on the floor by their looms doing this intricate work, and we do worry that the girls look very young as though they ought to be in school but are assured that is not the case.

The large showroom is filled with carpets made of silk, camel wool, best quality, lesser quality, subtle colours and brighter ones, every carpet taste catered for and every size too. We are seated and served green tea and sweet-meats, buttering the customer up being an essential part of the process. Of course, we are tempted to buy, but rational thought takes over, and we envisage our cats sharpening their claws and bringing up furballs on these delicate carpets and the idea of buying one fades. Some of our party do make purchases and can take the folded carpet with them or have it sent on.

Our retired politician purchases a carpet for his wife and has to give his name and address for the sending of the carpet. This is greeted with an exclamation "You are a Lord, and you've only bought a woollen carpet not a silk one!" His wife might be disappointed too – as she was also hoping for a silk carpet.

Then we are back on our aching feet to walk to an ancient market where there is some kind of festival taking place. Horsemen arrive and elegantly dismount, and their horses are taken off for stabling, but disappointingly no-one arrives on a camel. Our guide feels it necessary to tell us about the use of some wooden pipes on sale at a stall. He tells us that babies and young children have their arms bound to their sides in the cradle and a pipe inserted between their legs before their legs are bound together. The pipe drains into a pot below the cradle, and so there is no need for nappies. You will be glad to hear that there are different pipes for male and female babies.

The market is very lively with dancing and everyone wearing their best for the festivities, but what they are celebrating we never find out.

After we have walked through the market, no time to stop and buy on this occasion, we head off to see our last medressa of the day, now a craft centre, before finally making it to our hotel to shower and change.

We have been promised dinner in private homes, and for once that is exactly what we get. Our group is driven down an unpromising looking street, and we enter a door in a concrete wall that leads into a courtyard and find a tinkling fountain and small ornate pool. A table is set out with items for the preparation of the national dish, Plov, which

is traditionally cooked by the males of the household, but we are not clear whether the man wearing a chef's hat is their chef or our host. At any rate, he prepares the vegetables and meat with all the aplomb of a chef wielding a massive cook's knife.

The kitchen is by the side of the preparation area and separated from the rest of the house, much like kitchens of old that were away from the living areas of a house to avoid the risk of fire. The downside was that the food was always tepid by the time it reached the dining table.

We are told that this is an ordinary Uzbek household, but that doesn't look true for one moment. Before we head upstairs to the dining room, we need to remove our shoes to comply with local custom or put on blue plastic covers over them. The dining room itself is one of the most beautifully ornate rooms I have ever seen and also very new.

We have an intense debate about just how they have done the intricate white filigree work which covers the enormous mirrors. The room itself is so high that cleaning and dusting it with all the beautiful china on display in niches would take a team of monkeys a week or more. Mark, the dentist in our midst, declares that the filigree isn't a plastic moulding as most of us thought but plaster of Paris, which is what he is an expert on. The effect is stunning.

The Plov is very tasty, although some wonder whether the meat is indeed beef as we were told but instead perhaps horsemeat. Then it is back to our little hotel for another night.

CHAPTER SIX

Bukhara to Khiva

A rare day with no early rush to join the morning tour having been given some free time to explore the town by ourselves. We are so well trained that we leave the hotel before 9.00 in search of maybe some light retail therapy and a good cup of coffee. Such hopes are soon dashed as it is Sunday and the traders have not set up their stalls, and the few coffee shops remain firmly shut. So we wander aimlessly about in the largely empty town in the cool morning air.

We check out of the hotel by 11.00 to be transported back to the station and our waiting train. Some of our travel companions have sought to minimise the packing problem by using the hotel laundry service to recycle their clothes, but were somewhat snookered by the hotel having a major power cut the previous day (local construction workers severed the main electricity cable.) They do get their clothes back but un-laundered.

By 12.30 the train is underway, and we have lunch on board. The promised stunning landscape of the Karakum desert, wide steppes, blue skies and mountains is somewhat marred by the dull sunless day and jungle of telegraph wires and power lines spreading in all directions together with the misty conditions. The few roads are crossed by automatic level crossings which in addition to the usual barrier poles are equipped with the rising cams we sometimes see at carparks. It physically stops any car from crashing across the lines – installations that would prevent many

serious level crossing accidents if installed in the UK. The track is single with passing loops where we pass freight trains – these being something of a time warp as if the container revolution has never happened.

Anke, the tour director, gives us a lecture on the Silk Road over the radio first in English and then in German. She is a good lecturer and manages to sustain our interest. Otherwise, the hours are spent reading or chatting.

In the afternoon, the train comes to a stop at a wayside station in the middle of nowhere alongside a small very poor settlement whose only purpose is apparently to house the workers who maintain the railway. It is very primitive compared with the places we have visited so far, with privies in the backyard and also a cow or goat as a practical supply of fresh milk.

Informed that the stop is three hours, the only thing to do after photographing the loco, driver and train is to explore the muddy streets of the village, a huge contrast to the towns we have already visited. The only buildings of any substance are the small school and the station, the latter seems to be largely used for storing surplus furniture.

According to the station sign this place is called Karrakatta Stansiyasi. The rest of the sign appears to indicate the name of the train company operating the line.

It is interesting that English is the second language taught from junior school age, replacing the Russian taught before Independence. Also, the Cyrillic alphabet previously used for Uzbek has been replaced by the Latin alphabet. The attractions of the village are soon exhausted, and the train staff have prepared some light refreshments at the station, along with a whisky tasting which seems oddly inappropriate given the time and place.

Back on the train, it continues the long overnight journey to the station at Urgench the nearest to historic Khiva which is a 30-40 minute bus ride from Urgench. We are told that the railway is being extended to this ancient city and should open in a year or so.

CHAPTER SEVEN

Khiva

You have been travelling the Silk Road with us for a week now, and while we are approaching the highlights of our trip with visits to Khiva and Samarkand, the weather has deteriorated so no more blue skies and sunshine for the photos. Fortunately, unlike us, you cannot feel the biting wind and drenching rain that somewhat dampens the experience, although nothing could really detract from these wonderful sights which are magnificent in any weather. Our train is in the station at

Urgench which is the nearest station to Khiva. It isn't actually raining when leaving the train ("when the music starts…") and we are greeted by traditional dancers and musicians who smile broadly even at this early hour.

The welcome over, we join our cavalcade of minibuses with the usual police escort smoothing our way on the 45-minute drive to Khiva. I have to admit that I had never previously heard of Khiva, but it was once renowned on the Silk Road for slave caravans, with appalling desert journeys to reach it across steppes invested with brigands and bandits. It is an entire mud-baked walled medieval city, the best example in Central Asia. When we arrived in the cold drizzling rain, we simply walked back in time and are on a par with its former inhabitants. The undulating walls are massive and walking through them you are struck by the immediate sight of the Ichon-Qala, the inner walled city.

For the moment there are distractions as hat sellers galore are anxious to sell us Russian type fur hats against the weather. Many try them on, but few buy, as fur is a 'No, No' at home. At any rate, we are British and have our own raingear to protect us although it doesn't keep out the cold in the way that Russian garments would.

The city is said to have been founded by Noah's son who discovered a well here, and the original well can still be seen, if you search hard enough. There are after all more than sixty monuments, medrassas, minarets, museums and palaces here. It was a part of the Silk Road but a minor part. In recent centuries the city was subject to various Russian attempts to annexe it, usually ending in barbaric victories with thousands slaughtered but in 1873 the Russians did succeed in capturing it, and Khiva became a vassal state, and its silver throne was sent to Russia. The throne room is still here complete with replica chair.

The Ichon-Qala has four gates at North, East, South and West with the latter being the main entrance to the city. Much of the city has been the subject of restoration. There is an unfinished minaret which was built by a Khan in 1851, and it is said that he wanted to build a towering minaret from which he would be able to see all the way to Bukhara. Unfortunately, he died before it was finished and the building work stopped, leaving a beautiful short tiled structure waiting for someone to finish it. It was also realised that if the tower went any higher, it would give an excellent view of the palace and the Khans' harem!

The courtyard of the harem has four large apartments on the left for his official wives and a much larger number on the right for the women of the harem.

Outside the Kuhna Ark, the Khiva ruler's fortress, is a small building known as the Zindal or Khan's Jail, which houses all the torture instruments so that they were always handy if needed before execution in the palace square.

We enter a small ill-lit museum of the history of the area which is somewhat overcrowded because everyone seems to be taking shelter from the downpour. After ten minutes another guide looks in and turns on the lights which increased our interest in the exhibits no end now that we can see them. There are also fewer trip hazards when we can see where we are walking. Exiting the museum brings an exquisite tiled wall into view. It is so magnificent that we all stop, rain forgotten.

Wonderful buildings come into sight at each turn, and they take our breath away. If it had been sunny, we would have been completely

dazzled by the array of gilded minarets, domes, gateways, blue and white majolica tiles everywhere and the sheer height and ornateness of these monuments, medrassas, mosques and museums. They are totally stunning, but photographing these wonders of the world in the rain simply does not work. In earlier times some of the taller minarets had fires lit at night to act as a lighthouse to guide the caravans to the town.

There is one camel in the city, Katya, with whom tourists can have a photo opportunity but she's taking a lunch break when we come across her.

Khiva is planning to increase its tourist appeal with an information centre, hotel and cafes on a recently cleared site by the main gate entrance to the town plus the new rail link.

Eventually, we board our minibuses and drive back to the station at Urgench. Access to the station requires the production of a passport, but this is waived for our party, just as well as our passports are always being collected up for registration here and there. And there is our train waiting, we are home again.

CHAPTER EIGHT

Samarkand

We who with songs beguile your pilgrimage
And swear that Beauty lives though lilies die,
We Poets of the proud old lineage
Who sing to find your hearts, we know not why, –

What shall we tell you? Tales, marvellous tales
Of ships and stars and isles where good men rest,
Where nevermore the rose of sunset pales,
And winds and shadows fall towards the West:

And there the world's first huge white-bearded kings
In dim glades sleeping, murmur in their sleep,
And closer round their breasts the ivy clings,
Cutting its pathway slow and red and deep.

And how beguile you? Death has no repose
Warmer and deeper than the Orient sand
Which hides the beauty and bright faith of those
Who make the Golden Journey to Samarkand.

James Elroy Flecker

From school days the name Samarkand has conjured up the mysterious East and many exotic places that we children were never likely to go, but here we are after a lifetime of anticipation. We arrive through the hundreds of miles of desert sands by train, unlike those who journeyed of old. We are greeted on the platform by musicians and an invitation to use the VIP exit with the red carpet, totally undeserved of course, but we trip out along it anyway.

Samarkand dates back to the 5th century BC. It was once the capital of the Sogdian Empire – for those who watched the Silk Road series on TV – and was captured by Alexander the Great in 329 BC. When Alexander the Great first time saw Samarkand, he exclaimed: "I heard that the city was beautiful but never thought that it could be so beautiful and majestic".

Chinggis (Genghis) Khan wiped out the city in 1220 but the next conquering army to come along was that of Temur the Lame, or Tamburlaine, and in 1370 he decided to make the city his capital and rebuilt it. The city's importance has waxed and waned many times over the centuries, and it has, of course, suffered earthquakes, and finally, it was the Russians who restored its fortunes when they annexed it 1868 and built a railway connecting it to the Russian Empire.

We soon have our first sight of Registan Square. This is formed on three sides by towering medrassas with tilting minarets which have been partially restored first by the Russians and latterly by the Uzbekistan Government. These are the Tulugbek, Sherdor and Tilla Qori medrassas. The vast centre of the square was once filled with a lively bazaar selling all the wares for which the city was famous, metalwork, tiles, gold work, calligraphy and embroidery. Now the commerce has been cleared away only to resurface in all the nooks and crannies of the medrassas where sellers lurk to capture passing tourists, whether of Uzbeck or other nationalities, to sell their 'home-made' wares. It is incredible that the first of these medrassas was built in the 15th century and the last, not until the 17th, but now they appear as if they were built as one unit. One of the medrassas shows a mosaic of what appears to be a lion and a hind, but it is strictly forbidden in Islam to portray real animals so the artists claimed that they were purely mythical beasts and therefore acceptable.

Registran Square and its buildings are beautiful beyond the powers of description, but it is, of course, pouring with rain (and cold as well.) Our photographs were taken in these conditions so do not show the

beauty that would be evident in the sunshine with gleaming gold and turquoise domes and blue and white tiles lifted by the reflection of the sun. You will just have to use your imagination as we did. Not only are the external facades highlighted in gold, most of the inner courtyards and internal dome surfaces are also covered in gold as well.

After lunch, we check into the Grand Palace Samarkand Hotel where we will be staying for two nights. The name is, of course, grandiose and wholly inappropriate, but we do have a slightly larger room than in our poky Bukhara hotel, and much larger than our train compartment, all good. The folder in the room which normally details the amenities of the hotel only gives instructions on what to do in the event of an earthquake. Basically, there is nothing you can do but wait to be dug out.

Then off again to the Ulugbek's Observatory built on a small hill outside the city. The fact that we can visit this marvel is entirely down to a 20th-century Russian archaeologist, Vyatkin, whose dedication located the site and uncovered it in 1908. Ulugbek was a grandson of Timur, and in his turn became the ruler of the area but was more

famous as a mathematician and astronomer than as a ruler. He built his observatory in 1428 and was world-renowned for his learning. By the use of his observatory, basically a 45-foot radius quadrant half built in the ground and half above ground, he determined the length of the year to within one hour. Because his findings challenged the religious beliefs of the day he was assassinated in 1449 by religious extremists and his observatory razed to the ground. There is a small museum on the site explaining the significance or his work and placing him alongside other scientific minds of the era like Copernicus.

We finished the day at the Afroslab museum which displays important 7th-century frescos recovered from the palace of the Sogdian King Varkhouman. They show the king receiving ranks of foreign dignitaries astride elephants, camels and horses. These frescos were only discovered in 1965 and are one of the most important archaeological finds of recent years.

CHAPTER NINE

Samarkand
Day Two

The morning starts with a visit to a "factory" where high-quality handmade paper is produced from the bark of the mulberry tree in an age-old way. The twigs, which are a by-product of silk production, are stripped, the bark is boiled and pounded to a pulp and the sheets produced and dried, finally hand polished for ten minutes. While we are there a minor miracle occurs, the rain stops.

We have been told that this morning we will be visiting a Necropolis, it doesn't sound the most exciting visit and we imagine walking round tombstones in thick mud after the relentless rain. The reality is totally different. It is now brilliantly sunny, and there are a mere 284 steep, uneven steps for us to access the Necropolis. On the way, we have the opportunity to make new friends as the sun has brought out lots of Uzbek visitors many of whom want to be photographed with us for reasons we still don't understand.

This site is known as the Shai-I-Zinda complex and contains an avenue of palatial tombs dating back to the 11th century AD. The name itself means 'Living King' and legend has it that this refers to a cousin of the Prophet Muhammed who was injured by an arrow but did not die but was transported to Paradise while still living. There are of course many versions of the legend, some involving taking refuge in a well. The splendours of the forty-four tombs vie with one another in the richness

of their decoration. Wives of Temur are buried here and relatives of Ulabeg. We are told that visiting Shai-I-Zinda three times is equivalent to going on the obligatory pilgrimage (Hajj) to Mecca.

All religion was suppressed by the Russians during their long annexation of Central Asia. That did not stop them from repairing and restoring many of the ancient monuments which formerly had a religious purpose. While no-one practised any form of religion openly, it was not forgotten and surfaced again once they were no longer under the Russian yoke. So Islam is not of the fundamental sort here. It is not thought necessary for men to wear beards to be good Muslims. Women do not wear the hijab. Our guide for most of the trip is a Muslim but he, like most men of his age, only goes to the mosque twice a year. In a big city, men are more likely to attend the mosque for Friday prayers, but none of the Governments of these countries permits their employees to show any outward sign of practising religion, so there is no time off for daily or weekly prayers. We have only heard one call to prayer so far, and that was surprisingly in Turkmenistan. The medrassas here are mostly straightforward further education colleges rather than for religious studies. There are said to be ten medrassas in Uzbekistan, eight for boys and two for girls. The people know that it is their heritage to be Muslims, and the numbers of internal tourists show a keenness to embrace their roots, but religious fervour seems unlikely to flourish while Turkestan, Uzbekistan and Kazakhstan remain dictatorships. We had the impression that people are striving towards the more material aims of having the lifestyle of those in the Western world.

After the Necropolis we move on to a big market selling mostly food produce.

In the evening we visit Registran Square again to see it floodlit. A pity we weren't told about this visit as we only have one camera with us and the battery runs out after two photos.

CHAPTER TEN

Baysun Mountain Region & Shakhriabz

Checked out of the hotel and departed to the station by 8.00am. The train leaves at 8.45 with the opportunity of a second breakfast on the train as it travels towards the south-east. The day started cool at around 11 degrees and became sunny and warm during the middle of the day and then turned cold and wet during the afternoon and evening. After another lecture by our tour Manager to divert us during the morning, we enjoyed an early lunch at 11.15 on board the train.

After arrival at Kamashi we departed in our buses at 12.30 to a "typical" village where we are welcomed into the head man's house with music and dancing. Tables and chairs laid with light refreshments are set out in the garden and we are treated to a display of part of the local style of wedding celebrations with the bride and groom going round to each table greeting their guests. Then there are local dances where the Silk Road travellers are invited to join in.

The dances required more in the way of intricate hand and arm movements than fancy footwork. There was also a demonstration of how a baby was swaddled in a hanging cot – part of the equipment for which was described earlier. After friendship speeches and much tea (green or black) drunk, we departed in our coaches to Shakhriabz with the ever-present police escort.

After a 40 minute drive we arrive in the town which is celebrated

as the birthplace of Amir Temur (Marlowe's 'Tamburlaine'.) Our bus diverts to make a comfort stop at a local hotel where there is a band assembling to welcome visitors. But for once – it is not for us – they are waiting for some wrestlers to arrive at the hotel who are competing in the town at an international competition.

We proceed to the site of Amir Temur's palace. Although this is a World Heritage Site it is in danger of losing this status because of all the development work recently carried out. The massive entrance arches and some mausoleums remain, the whole site was engulfed by later town development. Recently the whole site has been cleared and the residents re-housed, the site is laid out as a large park surrounded by tasteful new development. A part of the original wall of the palace complex has been rebuilt with an entrance through the wall. We wander through the new park, which in twenty years or so will be a lovely shady place to stroll, photographing the monument to the Amir and the massive remains of the palace entrance, to the far end where the mausoleums await inspection. There is a mausoleum for one of the sons of Amir Temur who predeceased him. Close by is the mausoleum for the Amir – those of you awake at the back will of course remember that we have already seen the mausoleum to the Amir in Samarkand where he is indeed interred. However he always intended to be buried next to his son and had the mausoleum built in readiness. In the winter of 1404 he died far to the north and the winter was so severe that his body could not be brought over the mountain passes to his Palace in Shakhrisabz so in Samarkand he stayed.

While we had been on our visits, the train had moved to the station at Kamashi which was only a short drive away. Here it was intended that we have a barbeque on the platform produced by the train staff. Well, the cooking of the meat was done on the platform but the cold wet weather caused the serving and consuming to be transferred to the main station building. Surprisingly, this caused no inconvenience to the local travellers as absolutely no passenger trains arrived or departed in the seven or so hours our train was in the station!

The train departed after midnight for our next destination, Tashkent.

CHAPTER ELEVEN

Tashkent

Arrived at 10.13 with the usual musical greeting and then started our tour of Tashkent, the capital of Uzbekistan and the major regional centre of Central Asia. The sun is shining, and the temperature is around a pleasant 20°C all day. The first visit of the day was to the Khast Imom Square which is the official religious centre of the republic. The major historical interest is the Moyle Mubarek Library Museum which contains the 7th century Osman Quran which is said to be the world's oldest and was brought to Samarkand by Amir Timur. It was then taken to Moscow by the Russians in 1868 and returned to Tashkent by Lenin in1924. The library also displays more than thirty rare 13th-century books mainly Quran's.

Opposite the Library is the small Barak Khan Madrassa, now mostly filled with souvenir shops. We continued on to visit the Chorsu Bazaar, the large farmers market of Tashkent and also visited the nearby Kulkedash Medressa.

We also visited the memorial to the massive earthquake that occurred on 25th April 1966 which levelled large areas of the town. It shows the Russian builders who were drafted in to rebuild the city but who caused much resentment when twenty per cent of the new apartments were given to the Russians. The city's current look dates from the Soviet rebuilding after the quake but now has areas of post-independence improvements. The other striking feature is the cars on the road. Around ninety per cent are Chevrolets – not the be-finned gas guzzlers of the 60's American dream – but European/ Japanese style small saloons made by the local General Motors factory. Although petrol is very cheap in the three Stans, LPG is even cheaper at only a few pence per litre, and it is said that most cars are converted to run on

LPG. Most of the buses have some high-pressure gas cylinders on the roof to store the fuel.

Lunch was taken in an open-air restaurant. In the afternoon we walked past the Romanov Palace built in1891 by a cousin of the Tsar who was governor of the region. The palace is now used for official receptions by the Government. We then descended to the Metro for a short ride on one of the metro lines. The platforms were in a cavernous hall, very dissimilar to the London Underground. Our guide, a local, proved how infrequently he took the underground by mixing up which platform we needed. Eventually, we got it right and alighted near the Amir Timur Maydoni (Park) which was desecrated by the President without warning in 2010 when he ordered the clearance of the mature old trees, perhaps to show the new buildings around the park. The statue of Timur on horseback is now rather isolated, but the park itself still seemed popular.

Close by is the Mustaqillik Maydoni (Independence Square) where stone Pelicans guard the gateway. The Crying Mother Monument honours the 400,000 Uzbek soldiers who died in WW2.

The next event coming up, which we are all viewing with some trepidation, is a special performance of classical music given for the Silk Road travellers by the Uzbek State Academic Orchestra for Traditional Instruments. The venue is a small concert hall set out as though for a traditional classical concert. However, inspection of the instruments

shows that they are in no way the expected violins, cellos etc. but local traditional instruments that replaced their western classical counterparts. A lack of strings characterises the local replacements for violins, violas, cellos and basses. Given the musical welcome that we have received on arrival at some of the stations on the route, our expectations are not high, but it is a welcome opportunity to sit down for an hour. However, the orchestra turned out to consist of highly professional musicians who gave a spirited performance of some well-known classical works often showcasing strange solo instruments to great effect. The hour-long concert was received with a justified standing ovation at the end!

After dinner in a local restaurant we were taken back to the train for a 10.30 p.m. departure to the border, and the crossing into Kazakhstan which we are told will take some three hours in the night, but at least we stay on the train throughout.

After leaving Tashkent, it is a short 30-minute train ride to the border of Uzbekistan, but it takes three hours to cross into Kazakhstan. We are given strict instructions about this crossing. Firstly we have to fill out a Migration Card. Secondly, it is not permitted to take photographs at the border; thirdly we must stay in our cabins for the duration, tough if you have one of the cabins without toilet facilities.

We have previously been warned that some common prescription and even non-prescription drugs (e.g. paracetamol) are illegal in Kazakhstan with severe penalties for possession. After an hour at the Uzbek border at midnight, we are moved on to the Kazak border at 01.30 where some of the formalities are competed by the train staff, but each of us is photographed by two Kazak officials entering our compartment and taking photos of us in bed and mostly asleep. It takes another two hours, or so before the train moves on and we have been advised not to change into night clothes until the border formalities are completed. Fortunately, no inspection of our luggage takes place, or we could well have been there all night. Eventually, we get our duly stamped passports and Migration Cards back. The clocks also go forward by an hour, so we try and get some sleep for the rest of the night.

CHAPTER TWELVE

Turkistan, Kazakhstan

Turkistan contains Kazakhstan's greatest architectural monument and most important pilgrimage site. The Mausoleum of the first great Turkic Muslim holy man, Kozha Akmed Yasaui, was built by Timur in the late 14th century on a grand scale but was unfinished at the time of Timur's death and remains today bare of the tile work that adorns the rest of the building.

We arrive at 8.30, and for once there is no musical welcome. We depart in a police-escorted convoy the short distance to the historical site. We were told that some of our coaches and Kazak guides had been brought from up to 150 miles away to form the convoy for the trip to the site which is less than 10 minutes away. When we arrive only about three of the coaches are able to use the available car park after much careful positioning! They don't get many tourists other than Kazaks and few westerners visit here.

Our tour started with the Hivet semi-underground Mosque with a small cell to which Kozha Akmed Yasaui is said to have withdrawn towards the end of his life. He was born around 1103 and underwent ascetic Sufi training in Bukhara and lived there most of the rest of his life, having founded the Yasaui Sufi order, teaching in Turkistan and died in 1166. The cell he is said to have lived in can be seen in the corner of a room off the main Mosque. Next to the Mosque stands a wood pillared 19th century Friday Mosque although it is no longer used for worship.

After visiting a second semi-underground mosque, we continue to the main Yasaui Mausoleum. It is a very large structure containing thirty-five rooms which have many diverse uses. In one corner there is a Mosque with a beautifully tiled niche. It is said that it is one of a few mosques which allow women to pray alongside men.

Outside there is a partial reconstruction of the ancient walls and defences of the town, the site also has a collection of statues representing the silk road camel trains of the past.

We return to the train for lunch, and the train departs for the longest and last leg of our Silk Road Odyssey. The scenery viewed from the window is similar to the Uzbek deserts but slightly enlivened by passing small herds of firstly camels, then horses, cattle, sheep and goats all in the space of twenty minutes. In the afternoon we have a lecture about Kazakhstan to help pass the time. The container revolution has reached Kazakhstan as we pass a procession of container trains heading west.

Train travel seems to be more usual here with the public being able to access trains without the fuss of passports which are required in neighbouring countries. Stations that we pass through actually have people waiting for trains or waiting to sell things to passengers getting off trains, unlike in Uzbekistan and Turkmenistan. However, the Kazaks are slower than neighbouring countries in giving up the Cyrillic alphabet, but we are told that in about three years' time, they will also change to the Latin version.

Kazakstan is different to the other countries we have travelled through in that it is vast, the ninth largest country in the world but landlocked apart from the Caspian Sea in the East. Its population was last reported in 2017 as 18.6 million. Mostly the country is an empty nothingness of desert, but there are mountain ranges and green valleys of the Tian Shan, and on our train journey to Almaty the scenery changes from scrubby desert to green hills and mountains.

The capital is Astana, a newly built and futuristic city, but we head for Almaty a much more European type of city with wide leafy avenues and many parks in its centre.

This evening there is a farewell dinner on board the train with the usual presentations and speeches. The ladies wear their new Central Asian embroidered jackets or blouses as we all agree there is unlikely to be a suitable occasion to wear them at home unless we meet up for a reunion.

Then we retire to our compartments to enjoy the last night of our beds being shaken about by the Orient Silk Road Express. Perhaps we will miss this curious lullaby, who knows. As it happens, the train slows as it climbs to our final stop in the foothills of the Tian Shan mountains. so the shaking is less pronounced tonight.

CHAPTER THIRTEEN

Almaty

It might be the last day of this journey, but there is no let-up in the pace of the programme. After breakfast on the train we have a talk, via the radio, on the city we will be visiting while we struggle to clear the cubby holes, the safe and pack our suitcases one at a time due to the lack of space.

Almaty is the biggest city of Kazakhstan with a population of around two million people and until 1997 was the capital. The capital was then moved to the more centrally placed Astana by the newly independent government. Almaty has a large population of ethnic Russians (20-25%) and is culturally more diverse than any towns and cities visited on this trip. It is also a rich city since Kazakhstan, like Turkmenistan and Uzbekistan, has an economy underwritten by its oil reserves.

The city was founded in1854 by the Russians who did not like nomadic tribes as they were so difficult to govern. It was built on the site of an old Silk Road oasis called Almatu. The town was almost flattened by earthquakes in 1887 and 1911. In 1927 it became the capital of Soviet Kazakhstan with the name Alma-Ata (Father of Apples), and there are of course many stories about apples and why they are so important in the Kakastan culture. Apple orchards still flourish near the airport.

In 1930 the Turkestan-Siberia railway opened bringing big growth and prosperity. During WW11 factories were relocated from western

USSR where they were under threat from the Nazis, and many Slavs came to work in them. Ethnic Koreans were also forcibly resettled from the Russian Far East. In the 1970's & 80's the only Politburo member from central Asia managed to steer lots of money to his hometown of Almaty (renamed as such in 1991 after independence).

Almaty is situated on the northern foothills of the Tian Shan Mountains at an altitude of around one thousand metres. As the train slowly approaches the city, we pass the abandoned relics of the Soviet industrial era. The final destination is the Almaty 2 station. After passing Almaty 1, we slowly travel through the town alongside a road on the other side of which are located all of the car dealerships in the town. It could have been any western town as all the major European, and South East Asian manufacturers are represented – the cars on the road reflected the diversity of makes in contrast to the near uniformity in Uzbekistan. At 10.15 the train arrives, and after a final farewell to our cabin stewards, who have unloaded our cases to be sent straight to the hotel, we form up in our groups for the morning tour.

We now have a new guide called Svetlana, who in spite of her youthful appearance seems to have been trained in the old Soviet Intourist mode. She is determined that we will see everything that Almaty has to offer, whether we want to see it or not.

The main stop of the morning is the Orthodox Ascension Cathedral which is one of the largest wooden buildings in the world. It was built in 1904 and survived almost undamaged by the 1911 earthquake. It is currently undergoing some repairs and covered in scaffolding. Internally it is decorated with many icons which had been hidden during the early Soviet era. After the clean lines of the many mosques visited, the overall effect is very depressing to anyone not brought up in the Orthodox/Catholic tradition.

Just to the east of the Cathedral is the War Memorial in Panfilov Park. The park is named after an Almaty Infantry unit in which 28 heroes died fighting off Nazi tanks in a village outside Moscow in 1941. The memorial depicts soldiers from all 15 soviet republics bursting out of a map of the USSR. An eternal flame honouring the fallen of the 1917-20

(Civil War) and 1941-45 (WW11) flickers in front of the giant black monument. After lunch, the tour continues by coach ascending into the Tian Shan Mountains to the winter sports centre fortunately without snow at this time of year. This is situated at an altitude of 700 metres (2200 feet) above Almaty. At the first winter Olympics after WW11 the Russians did very badly, and Stalin decreed that a new base should be established to train athletes for future competitions. After an exhaustive search throughout the USSR this site was chosen as having the best combination of snow, weather and accessibility and for many years this was the main location for Russian training of winter sports athletes. The main installation is the Ice skating arena and a ski lift to reach higher up into the mountains plus accommodation for the athletes. It was, of course, closed as the winter is over so we could only look at the outside of the ice rink. As usual, no coffee stop or lingering allowed.

The locals are very proud of the fact that in the Tian Shan Mountains above Almaty there are believed to be about 300 of the endangered snow leopards living. The snow leopard is one of the symbols of Almaty.

We had hoped to be taken up the snow-covered mountains to enable us to look at the view, but no such luck.

After the afternoon tour, we check into our hotel for a brief rest. This is a luxury hotel with a large bedroom and large bathroom, and in case we are suffering withdrawal from a lack mosaics in the day's tour – it has a mosaic over the bath. Unfortunately, we will only be spending a couple of very short periods in the hotel – barely time to even risk closing our eyes for a few minutes in case we miss the next stage of the tour.

The details of the final outing had been kept vague – as indeed many of the other outings had a fair share of surprises. This one was simply described as the "farewell dinner in a traditional yurt restaurant". Our coaches drove us into the city and stopped and dropped us off on a busy road with no sign of a restaurant or a yurt. We walked a few hundred yards to a cable car station where we were sent, six at a time, for a six-minute ride up what the locals called the green mountain (Kok-Tobe), an 1100 metre hill on the city's southeastern edge. From the top, there are great views over the city and the mountains, plus an assortment of attractions. I am immediately called to order by Svetlana when I break away to take a photo of the stunning view. Independent viewing is not allowed.

Being a Sunday evening, it was busy with locals enjoying the attractions. These included a Ferris wheel, roller coaster, children's playground, craft shops, cafes and restaurant and a life-sized bronze statue of all four Beatles installed in 2007 and claimed to be the only one of all four in the world. Locals were queuing up to have their pictures taken sitting amongst the "Fab Four". We were told that during the summers in the late 1960's and early 70's all you could hear coming out of the open windows in the city were Beatles hits. Surprising, since this was before English was regularly taught as the second language in schools.

The 'traditional yurt' restaurant turns out to be a large modern concrete structure with no discernible resemblance to a Yurt, and this is where we have our final farewell dinner. Like most of the other meals off the train, it was not memorable and only notable for offering the option of horsemeat. (Most declined – it looked rather fatty.) And it was our last opportunity to have chak-chak, whose popularity has spread from the Uzbeks to the Kazaks. Dining takes place against a background of loud Kazak pop music which is as painful to our ears as that of the pop music of Turkmenistan and Uzbekistan. Authentic local music would have been fine, but this noise is only good when it finishes. Getting old? Us?

We had no idea when we started this journey quite how many mosques, medrassas and mausoleums we would visit and do wonder whether there can be any left in Central Asia that we haven't seen. You will all know how tour guides are so proud of their countries that they insist on visitors seeing everything, without exception. We had hoped to see at least some preserved Caravanserai but any that survived were all turned into Medrassas centuries ago. There have been many surprises along the way, mostly good ones, nothing is ever quite what is expected. We're glad to have made this trip but quite exhausted.

We have travelled over 2500 miles by train and if you have tried to follow our journey on a map, you will probably have admitted defeat. There are so many different spellings for every place we have visited, and many of them are simply not shown on even our recent map of Central Asia. As we have been travelling by train, our routes have been a bit tortuous with plenty of doubling back along a railway track already travelled. Likewise, the spelling of the names of rulers of this region varied each time we've seen them written, so apologies for any apparent inconsistencies.

CHAPTER FOURTEEN

Recipes

CHAK-CHAK

This is a favourite Uzbek dessert and was originally cooked on Eid, but it has become so popular it is now cooked all the year round. It will keep for 2 weeks and is crispy and sweet.

Ingredients to serve 6:
6 eggs
a pinch of salt
1 ½ tbs of vodka or cognac
Flour as needed
3 cups vegetable oil for frying
1/3 cup sugar
100 gm water 1 cup honey
Toasted almonds (optional)

Separate egg whites from yolks. Beat egg yolks with a mixer until they are light in colour. Separately beat egg whites until it forms stiff peaks. Very carefully mix whites and yolks, add salt, and vodka. Carefully start adding flour gradually mixing in between until all the flour has been absorbed. Leave for 15 minutes.

Slice into 6 pieces, and spread the oil on both sides. Cut into strips 1.5 inches wide, and cut the strips into short sticks.

Heat the oil in a deep frying pan, put in the short sticks and fry until a light golden colour.

In a deep pan put all the sugar and water, and make the syrup. To check the readiness of the syrup: just put some drops of on to the back of a chilled plate. Then add in honey and simmer for 4-5 minutes but don't over boil. Pour the syrup over the fried sticks while hot and carefully mix it with a wooden spoon.

Decorate with seeds or chocolate chips or whatever you fancy or toasted almonds.

To store wrap in foil. Do not refrigerate.

~~~~~~

PLOV

This is the national dish of Uzbekistan, and there are hundreds of different regional variations on how to make it. It is traditionally cooked by the men of the family, this presumably works the same way as men cooking on a barbecue or Spanish men cooking paella over an open fire with all the preparation done by the women and the last showy bit done by the men who then receive all the compliments.

Ingredients to feed 6:
½ cup vegetable oil
2 large onions
1 ½ lb lamb or beef
1 lb Basmati rice
1 lb carrots
1 tbsp cumin seeds or powder
1 tsp coriander
1 head of garlic
Salt & pepper

Peel and slice onions. Peel and cut carrots into two-inch sticks. Cut meat into cubes. Fry onions until brown and then add meat and fry on high heat. Add carrots and cook for another ten minutes. Add cumin, coriander, salt and pepper and 4 cups of water. Bring to boil. While it is coming to the boil take some of the skin off a garlic head and slice the top of it. Add it whole to the boiling mixture then turn down to simmer for an hour with a lid on the pan.

After an hour add the rice with 3 more cups of water and mix in. Cook for another 30 minutes until liquid fully absorbed. When cooked let it rest for 15 minutes before serving.

CHAPTER FIFTEEN

Visas

Most nationalities are required to obtain visas to visit the Silk Road countries. This is not an easy process and you are advised to use a visa agent, Visa Central, part of the CIBT Group, is the preferred partner for the Consulates for these former Soviet countries. Even so there is a lot to do to get your visas and it is not cheap. As a lawyer I am used to form filling but the application forms drove me to distraction. It took me an age to realise that addresses and other information had to be entered backwards, that is postcode, county, town, street, number etc. Some of these are filled out online and then need to be printed out and either delivered by you directly to the consulate or sent to a visa agent to do it for you. The consulates are not open every weekday and close at will on days when you expect them to be open. The application has to be delivered by hand and then picked up days later. You will need some current passport type photos and numerous copies of the relevant pages of your passport.

Turkmenistan

The whole process starts with the necessity for a letter of invitation from a travel agent in Turkmenistan which has been certified by the State Migration Service. Your travel agent will provide this for you. It is a precious document which must accompany your visa application. The whole process costs serious money.

When you arrive at the airport in Turkmenistan you will also have to fill out an immigration form, with more photos and passport copies and a fee payable in local currency. It is a lengthy process. After that you must register with the State Service of Turkmenistan for Foreign Nationals within three days of arrival. If you are travelling with a tourist group they will deal with this for you.

Uzbekistan

They have just introduced a trial of an electronic visa which will be valid for a period of up to thirty days. The visa will be valid for 90 days from the date of issue so do not apply too early. As this visa will not be endorsed on your passport you will need to print out a paper copy or carry it in electronic form or both. A transit visa valid for five days has also been introduced if you will be simply passing through to visit another of these landlocked countries. There are also exit forms to complete.

Kazakhstan

Until 31st December 2018 citizens of the UK, EU, Australia, America and Canada may enter the country for 30 days without applying for a visa first and without an official letter of invitation. Your day of arrival counts as Day One.

On entering Kazakhstan, you will be asked to complete a white registration card and present it to the border officers, who will stamp and return to you with your passport. They will also photograph you. You must retain this registration card during your stay and present it when departing Kazakhstan. If the card has two stamps, you are registered with the Migration Police for up to 90 days. If the card contains only one stamp, you must register with the Migration Police within five calendar days. Certain hotels throughout Kazakhstan are also able to register foreign guests.

Be sure to carry your passport with you at all times as you may be required to produce it on demand at any time. You may be taken in for questioning if you don't have your passport with you or if you take pictures of certain buildings or other sensitive infrastructure. Penalties for violating registration rules, including failing to produce a white registration card on demand, are heavy.

Earthquakes

Turkmenistan, Uzbekistan and Kazakhstan are all earthquake-prone countries. In particular the earthquake threat level within the Almaty region is Level 4 (the highest level assigned). Building practices do not generally meet seismic standards elsewhere and be warned that local authorities do not have sufficient resources to respond to a large-scale disaster.

General

There are problems with taking your prescribed and over the counter tablets with you. Carry prescription medication in its original packaging, along with your doctor's prescription. There are many over the counter drugs which are not legal in Kazakhstan and you are advised to check the regulations carefully before travelling as penalties for possession are severe.

Read everything you can about local customs and practices in these countries so that you don't inadvertently offend.

COMING SOON

BOOK TWO IN THE SERIES

Travelling in Vietnam and Cambodia

Printed in Great Britain
by Amazon

46275722R00059